Performing Guitarists
Tricks & Licks

How to Sound Like the Song

Easiest Way to Up Your Game

A Straight Line to Get There

Best Investment of Your Time

PerformingGuitarists <u>youtube.com</u>

performingguitarists@gmail.com

Copyright © 2021 by **Perry D Howell**

Description

This Guitar Chord Inversion and Scale Book will help Performing Guitarists playing Rock, R&B, Soul, Country, Blues, Gospel and Jazz songs as a single, duo or band, making your guitar performance stand out by playing all the right parts. In 2 to 3 seconds, before the singing starts, the listener should know the song !

"How To Sound Like the Song."

If you are a music writer, arranger or singer and performing live, this book will help you better showcase your product. Play the right part at the right time and you will always sound better. It is not about the guitar part.

"It is about what the listener hears."

At any one point in a song something stands out and that is what should be played. The part may be the bass, keyboard, horns, guitar or strings but that's the part to play. This book will give you what you need to know to be a good working guitarist. It will make your guitar and your singing sound better. This book will also make music theory on guitar easy. The practice guide well develop your guitar technique with chord inversion and scales.

"The Better You Sound - The Better You Sound!"

Elevate your show!

Table of Contents

Chapter 1:   **Basic Music Theory on Guitar**

    What is Music Theory and How it Works on Guitar?

Chapter 1:1 **How Music Theory Works on Guitar**

    A logical and practical way to learn guitar is with a step by step program.

Chapter 1:2 **The Math of Basic Music Theory**

    Basic Math formulas for Music are easy.

Chapter 1:3 **Each String is Divided into Half Steps.**

    Open to the Twelfth fret is an Octave

Chapter 1:4 **Fingerboard Logic**

    Hearing and Visualizing the fingerboard

Chapter 2:   **Understanding Chords on Guitar**

Chapter 2:1 **Basic chords by string groups- 12 basic chord shapes**

    1st set of 3 Note Chord Inversions Major & Minor with Arpeggios

    2nd set of 3 Note Chord Inversions Major & Minor with Arpeggios

    3rd set of 3 Note Chord Inversions Major & Minor with Arpeggios

    4th set of 3 Note Chord Inversions Major & Minor with Arpeggios

Chapter 3: Understanding Scales on Guitar

Chapter 3:1 Scale Forms

    2 String Scales Major & Minor & Pentatonic

    3 String Scales Major & Minor & Pentatonic

    4 to 6 String Scales Major & Minor & Pentatonic

Chapter 3:2 Harmonized Scales

    Scales in 3rds

    Scales in 6ths

    Scales in Octaves

    Scales in 10ths

Chapter 3:3 Diatonic Harmonized Scales

    Harmonized Scale Major, Minor, Blues, Pentatonic, ect....

    Chords placed on each step of the scale

    A scale chord can make transitions much more expressives.

Chapter 4: Copy Players you like. You will learn faster.

    Five players you like.

    Finger Style you like

    Pick Style you like

    Pick and Fingerstyle you like

Chapter 5: Pedal Tones

Chapter 5:1 What is a pedal tone?

Chapter 5:2 Why would you use it?

Introduction

About Building Your Music Vocabulary

It is no surprise that we find all of these chord voicings combined throughout commercial music styles. It is because they are recognizable as standard vocabulary. This vocabulary is some of the most popular and common guitar chord voicings in commercial music.

The key with most chord changes is the least movement is the best. You want to sound like a thinking artist. Play the sample vocabulary just enough to understand it and move on.

Don't lose momentum! Hopefully learning with this book will be easy and fun. Magic is only magic when you don't know how it's done. Now look behind the curtain!

For the most part all of these common chord tone licks are based around chord inversions. Where do all these ideas come from ? I have grouped sound phrases together to show different song styles with the same chord inversions as the basis for their songs.

KISS = Keep it Simple Stupid !

What would a music vocabulary look and sound like?

1: Chords - used in a style of music. All styles have recurring chord progressions.

2: Scales - used in a style of music. Pentatonic, Blues, Major, Minor, Modes ect..

3: Arpeggios - used in a style of music from travis picking to sweep picking ect...

4: Rhythms - used in a style of music where the beat is placed.

5: Lick & Trick - for each style of music, octave, 3rd, 6th, ect...

6: Your personal style - Picking the tools for what you like to play.

All musicians have their own vocabulary, some just bigger!

There are so many books out on music, just where do you start?

This is just a small sample but hopefully it will get you started.

Keep in mind not all of the information in this book is needed to

play well and entertain others but it never hurts to

Raise The Bar!

"Never stop learning because that is what makes life fun"

Where Music Magic Happens

Build the Vocabulary You Want

Make Your Own Music Magic

Once you know all 12 chord inversions, all mainstream music will become easier to play. We are only looking at 12 basic chord shapes and their variations.

Your ability to hear what happens in a song will be so much sharper. It will make playing music more fun and rewarding.

You will also notice all the big bar chords you know are made of small chord inversions stacked on top of each other. The big 6 string chords are not as easy to manipulate, and generally do not represent the song. This is by no means advanced knowledge, but what I believe a good working guitarists needs to know.

How to Learn Chord Inversions

Take a song you already know well and find different ways to play it on each set of 3 chord inversions. You will find that playing the song this way will help you hear parts of songs you were missing.

This is an easy and fun way to learn what good working guitarists do. Keep each step small and repeat until easy.

Samples of Chord Inversion Licks

We first start with samples of what you might do with a chord inversion vocabulary.

These samples of common chord inversion sounds are used by everyone.

If you didn't already know this information, well now you do. Once you

understand chord inversions you will find sounding like the song easy.

You can see from the sample chord inversion licks how much sound you get

from chord inversions.

How much you develop your vocabulary will depend on how many styles you wish to play.

No matter what your music taste, this will be a very fun way to dig in and sound like a pro.

No longer will you wonder what the keyboard players and horn players are doing.

All parts can be played by you. Don't think small and strum big chords, think big and

play small chords.

Samples of Chord Inversion Licks

Phrasing in 3rds

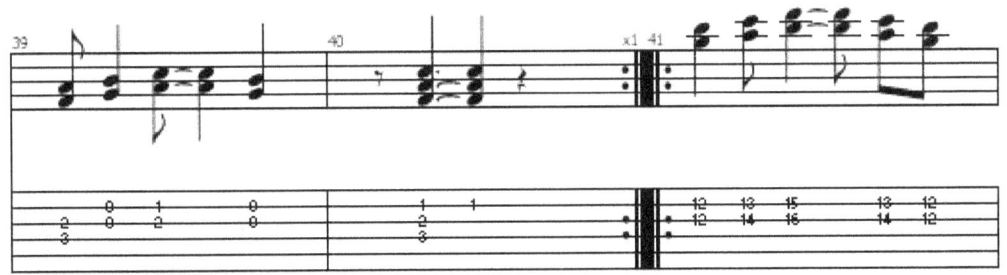

Phrasing in 10ths

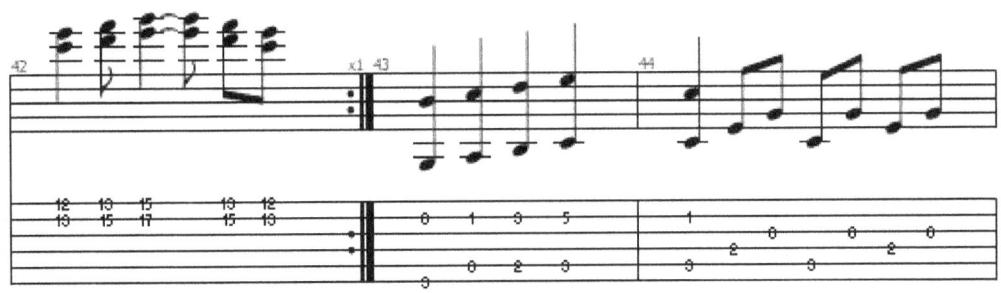

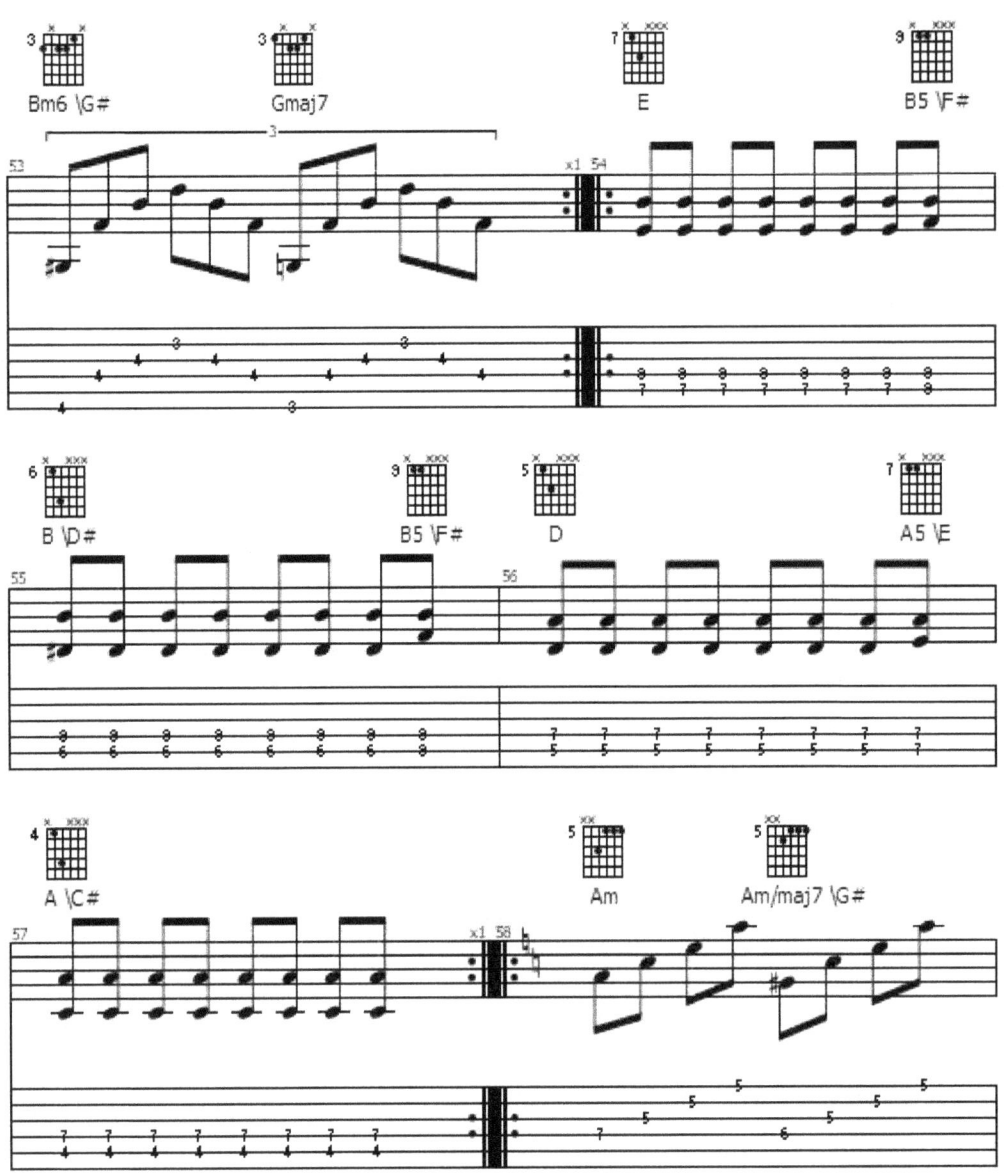

Chapter 1

Chapter 1: Basic Music Theory on Guitar

What is Music Theory and How it Works on Guitar?

Theory is a way to understand what you played or heard so you can do it again. What does that mean? It means if you know what made it work, you can make it work most anywhere (not counting for bad taste) . If one knows a melody starts on the 5th of a chord then you can start it on any chord.

Chapter 1:1 This Book is How Music Theory Works on Guitar.

A logical and practical way to learn guitar is with a step by step program. Taking the guitar in small bites will help us stay the course. This is by no means the only way to see the guitar but it is a system. This system is based in standard music teaching. This will help guitarists who are working with people who are not guitarists.

Chapter 1:2 The Math of Basic Music Theory

Basic Math formulas for Music are easy. Scales have formulas and chords come from them as do chord progressions. The math for a major scale is whole/whole/half/whole/whole/whole/half step. This means we can play a major scale on any one string. To keep it simple, chords are every other note in a scale. Example: Root chord = 1 note, 1st inversion = 3rd note and 2nd inversion = 5th note of scale.

Chapter 1:3 Each String is divided into Half Steps.

Open to the Twelfth fret is an octave. A whole step on the guitar is two frets and a half step is one fret. This makes it easier to see chord inversions on the guitar, by spelling the chord on one string.

Chapter 1:4 Fingerboard Logic -

Hearing and Visualizing the fingerboard.

The ability to automatically translate sounds in your head into shapes on guitar is a must. Octaves-Tenths- Sixths- Thirds- and chord inversions must be recognized . Play with your inner ear !

CHAPTER 2

Chapter 2: Understanding Chords on Guitar

Foundation and imagination go hand in hand. Working with chord inversions will give you great ear training and open your imagination!

Chapter 2:1 How to Practice Your Chord Inversions.

Take a song you already know and play it on the first set of three strings in a four fret range, in three different positions on the neck. You just learned how to play most of your songs in a new way. Play the same song now in a new key. Do the same thing with each of the four sets. Then mix sets, 1 & 2 then 2 & 3 and 3 & 4.

Now what you're looking for is to play a song with the least amount of movement from one chord to another, this gives your song arrangement a smooth and connected feel.

Remember less is more, find the groove!

This is the best ear training ever!

Chord Inversion 1st set of 3 Major and Minor
(Chord Inversion 1st set of 3 Sus4 and Dominant7th Sus4)

Chord Inversion 1st set of 3 Major Minor Arpeggios

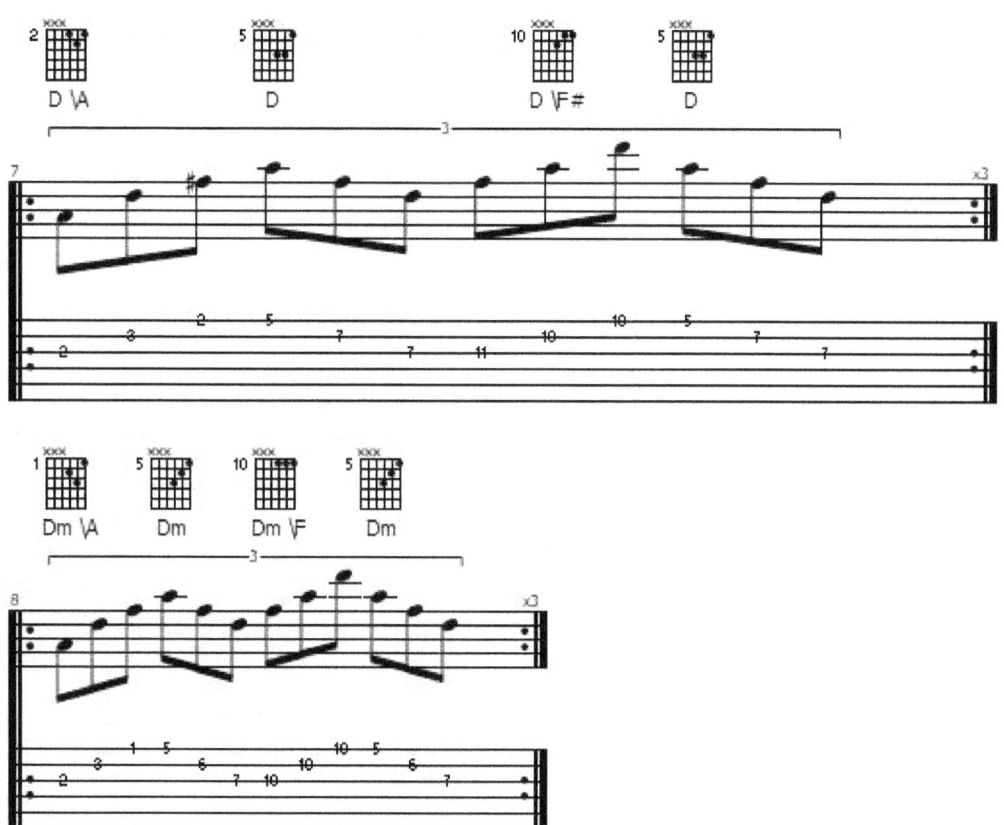

Set 1 Harmonized Scale Chord Inversion

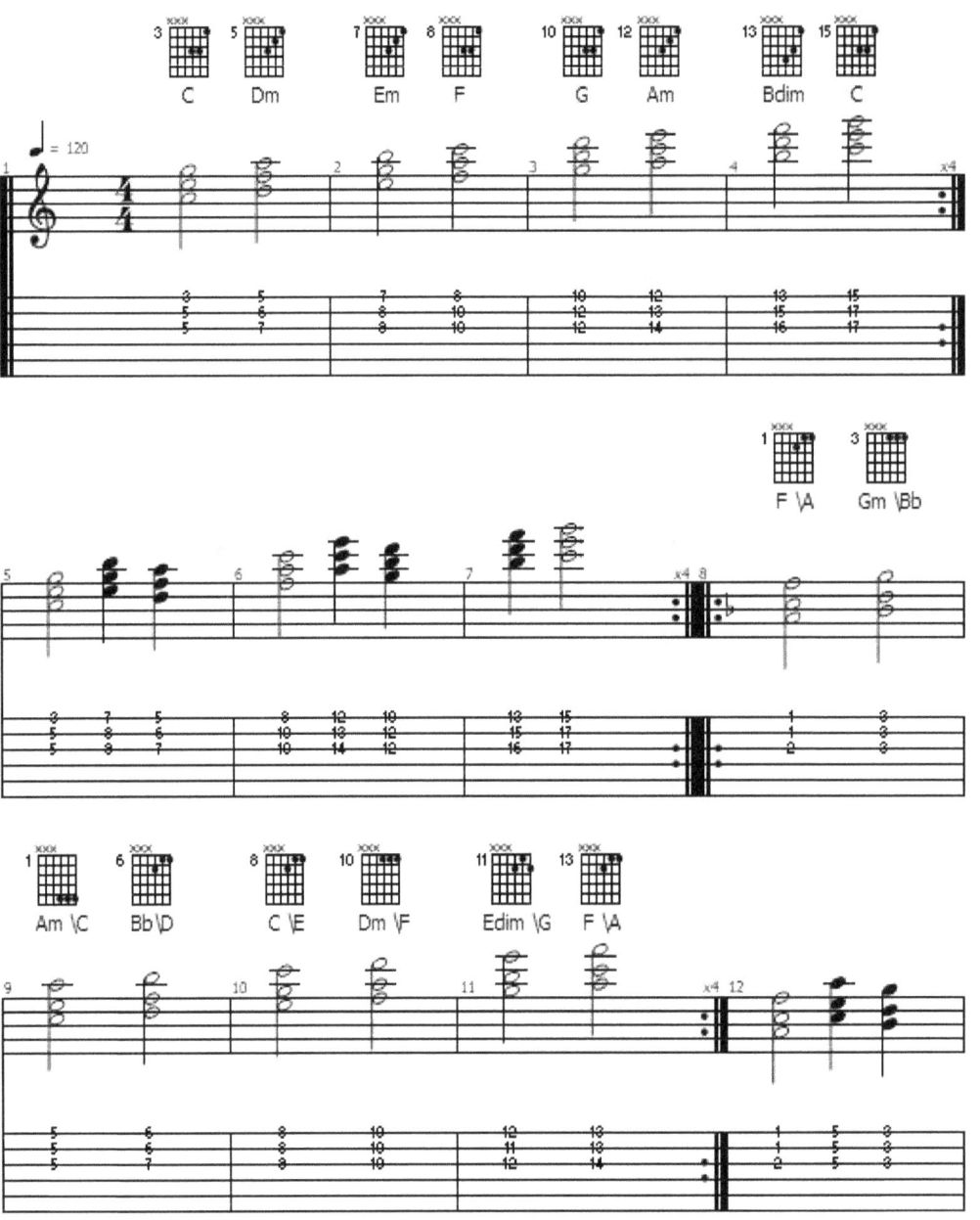

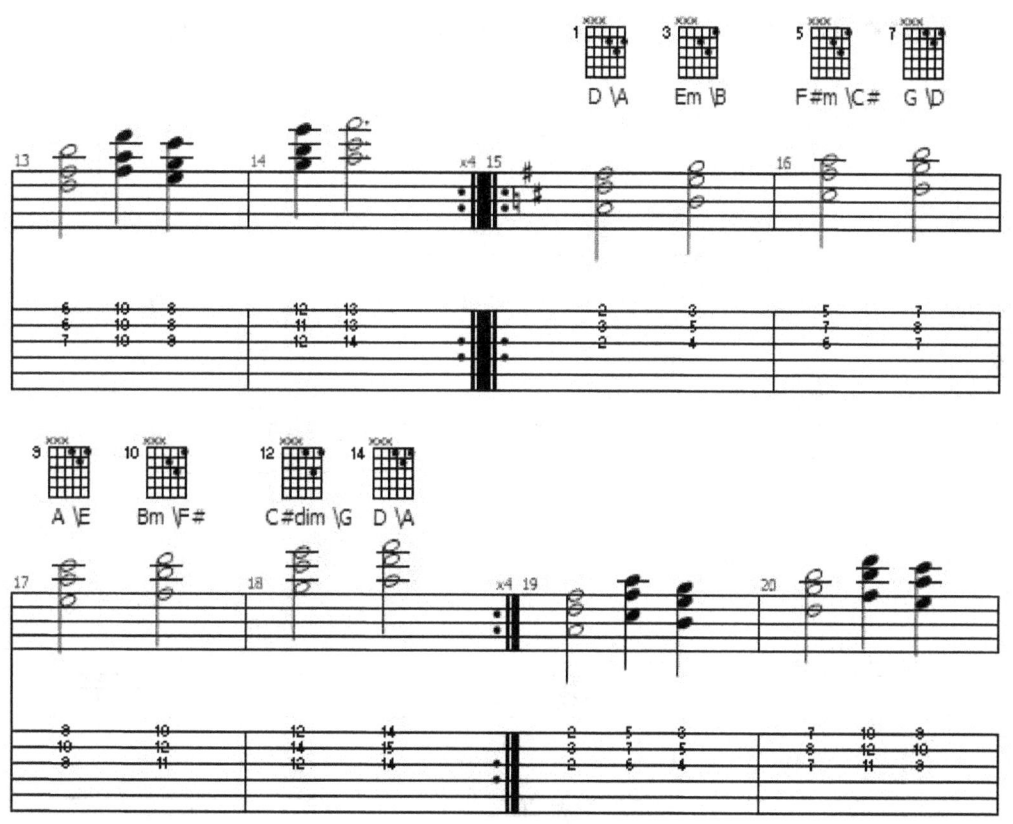
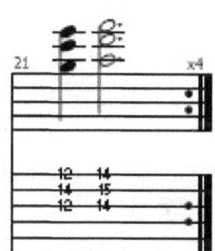

Chord Inversions 2nd set of 3 Major and Minor

(Chord Inversions 2nd set of 3 Sus 4 and Dominant 7th Sus 4)

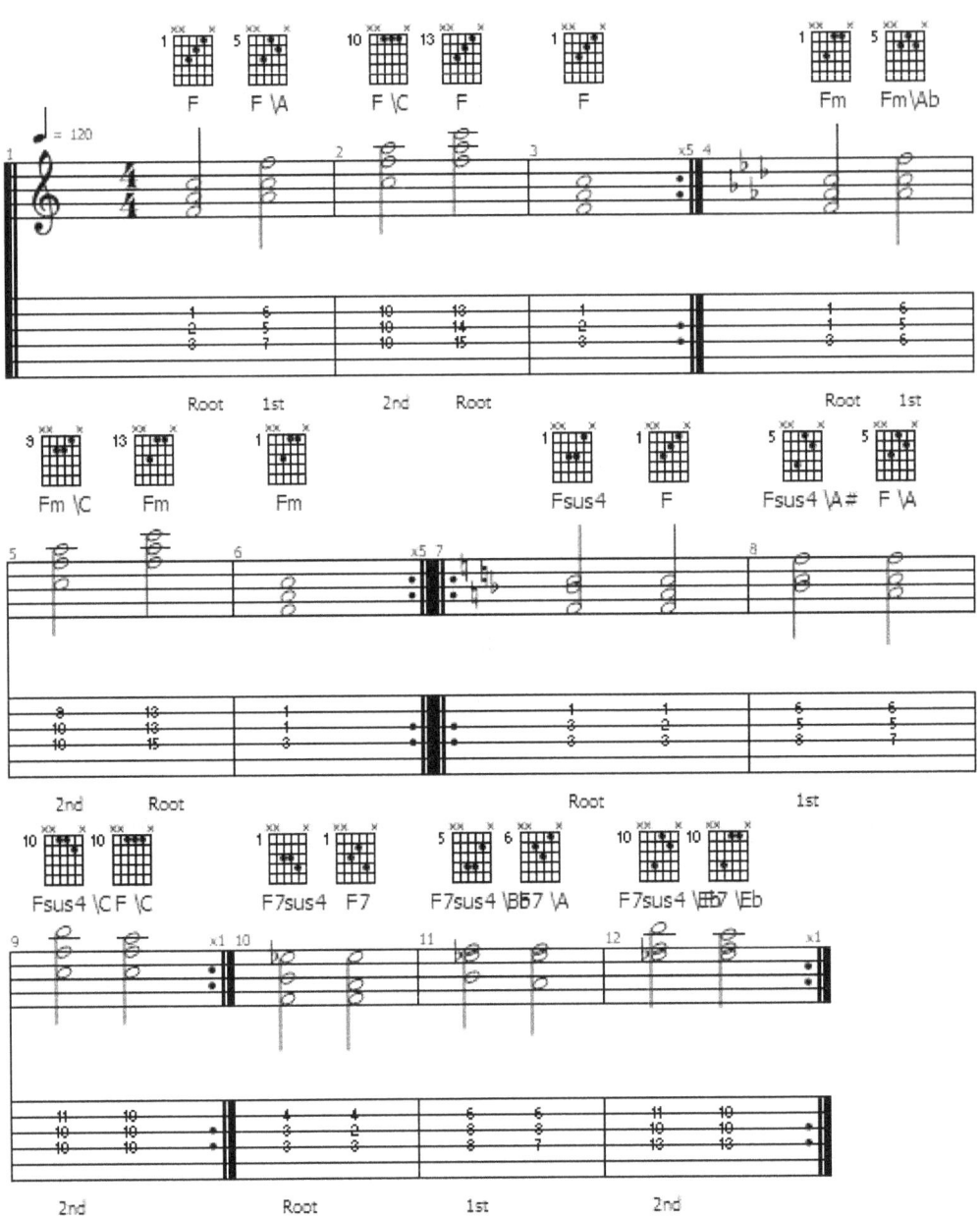

Chord Inversions 2nd set of 3 Major Minor Arpeggios

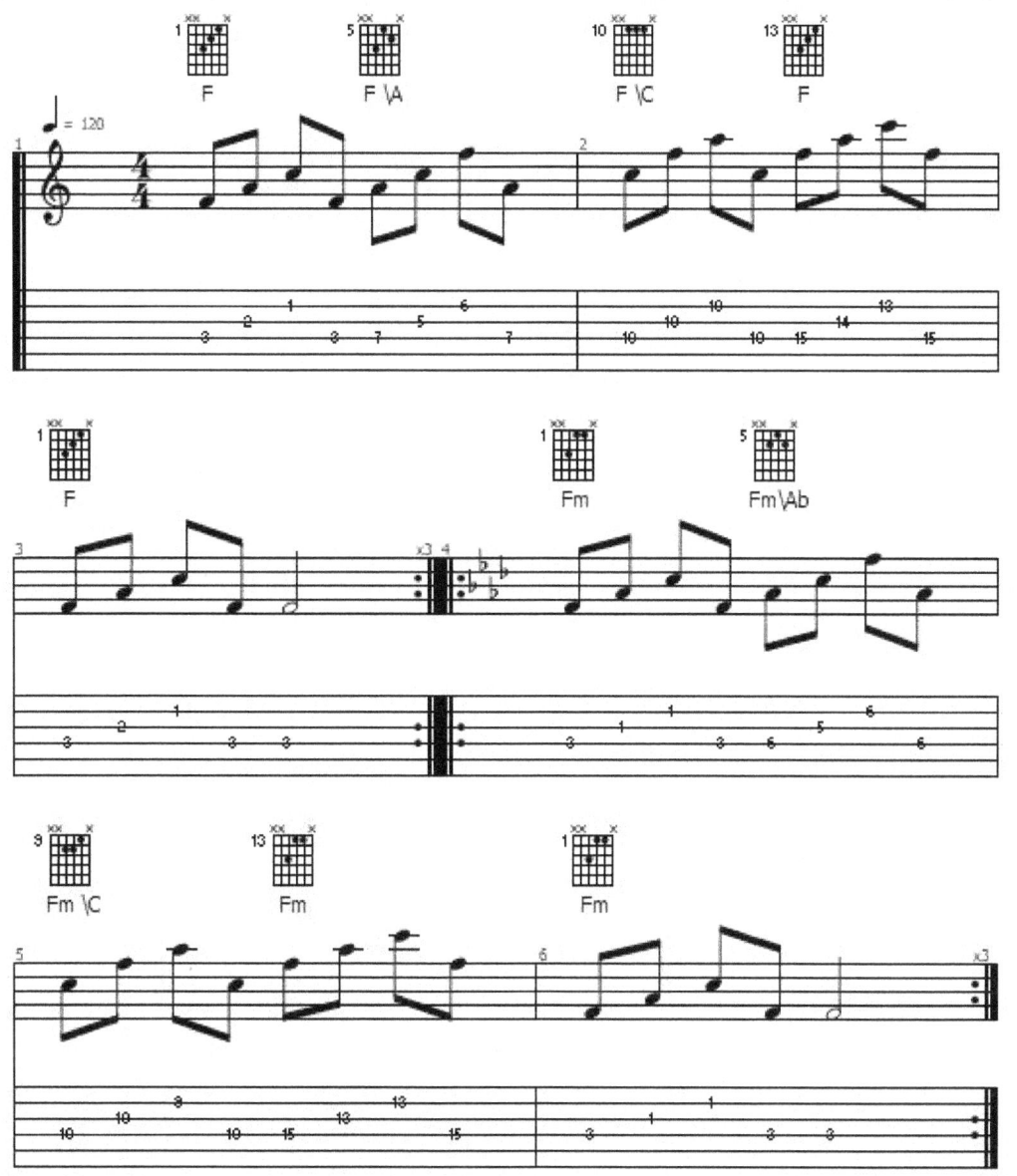

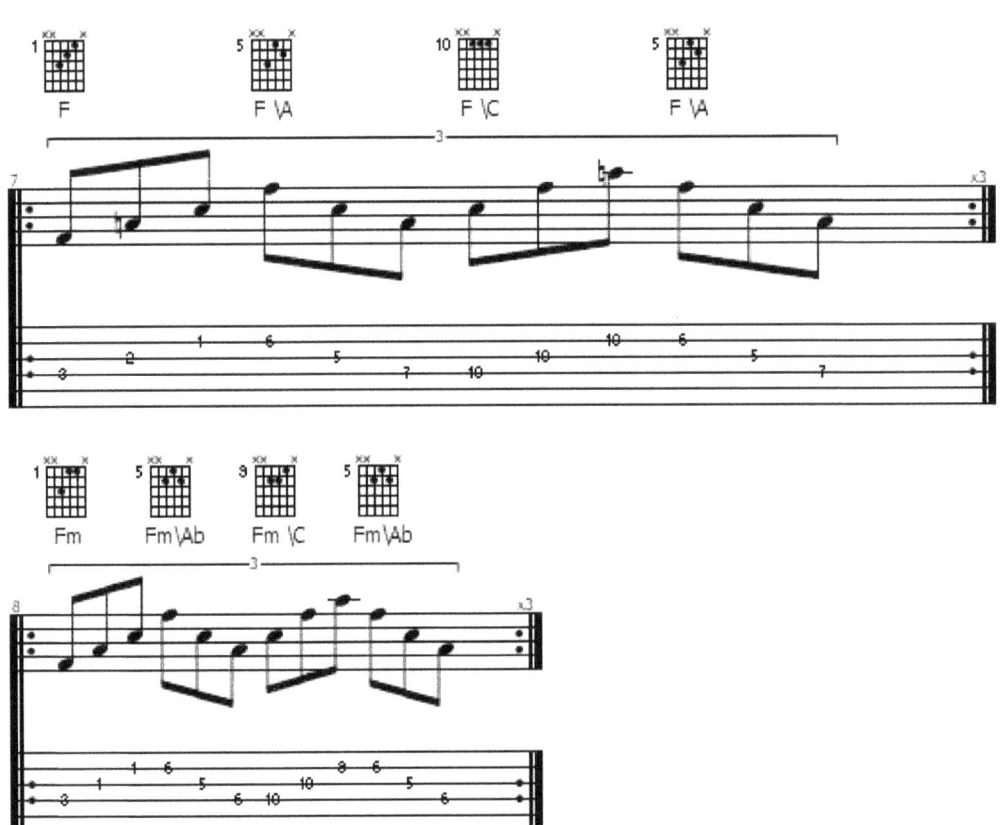

Set 2 Harmonized Scale Chord Inversion

Chord inversions 3rd set of 3 Major and Minor
(Chord Inversions 3rd Set Major Sus 4 and Dominant 7th Sus 4)

Chord Inversions 3rd set of 3 Major Minor Arpeggios

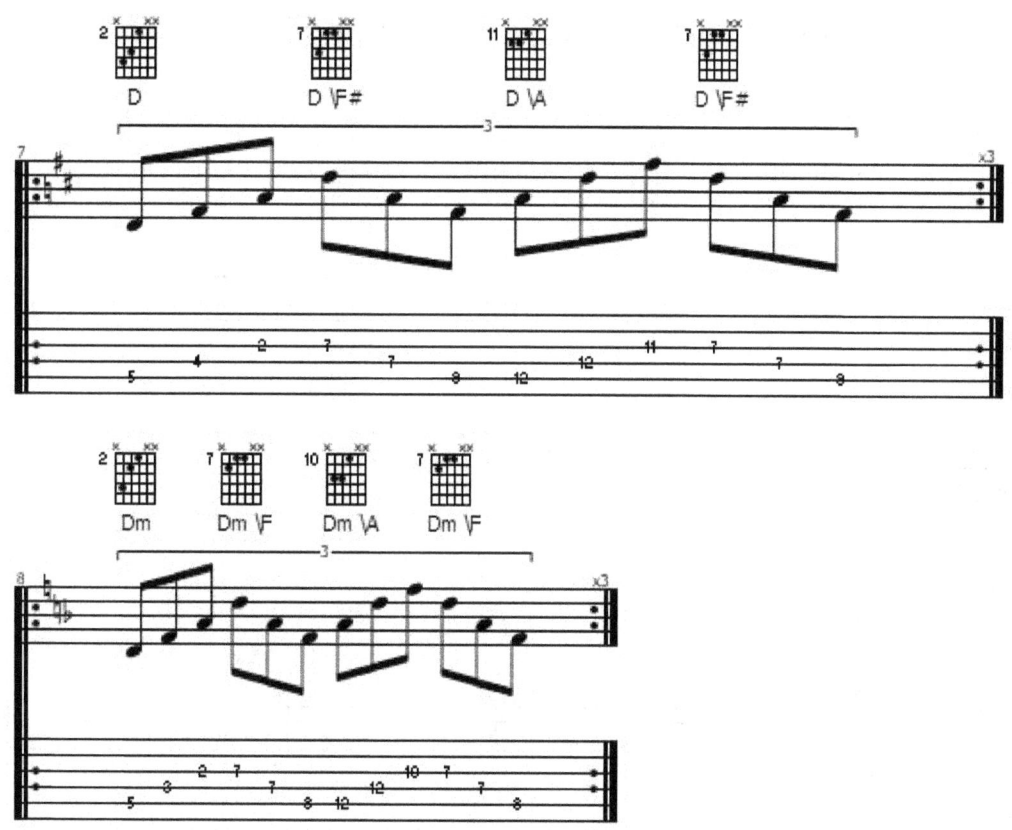

Set 3 Harmonized Scale Chord Inversion

Chord Inversion 4th set of 3 Major and Minor

(Chord Inversion 4th set of Major Sus 4 and Dominant 7th Sus 4)

Chord Inversion 4th set of 3 Major Minor Arpeggios
( )

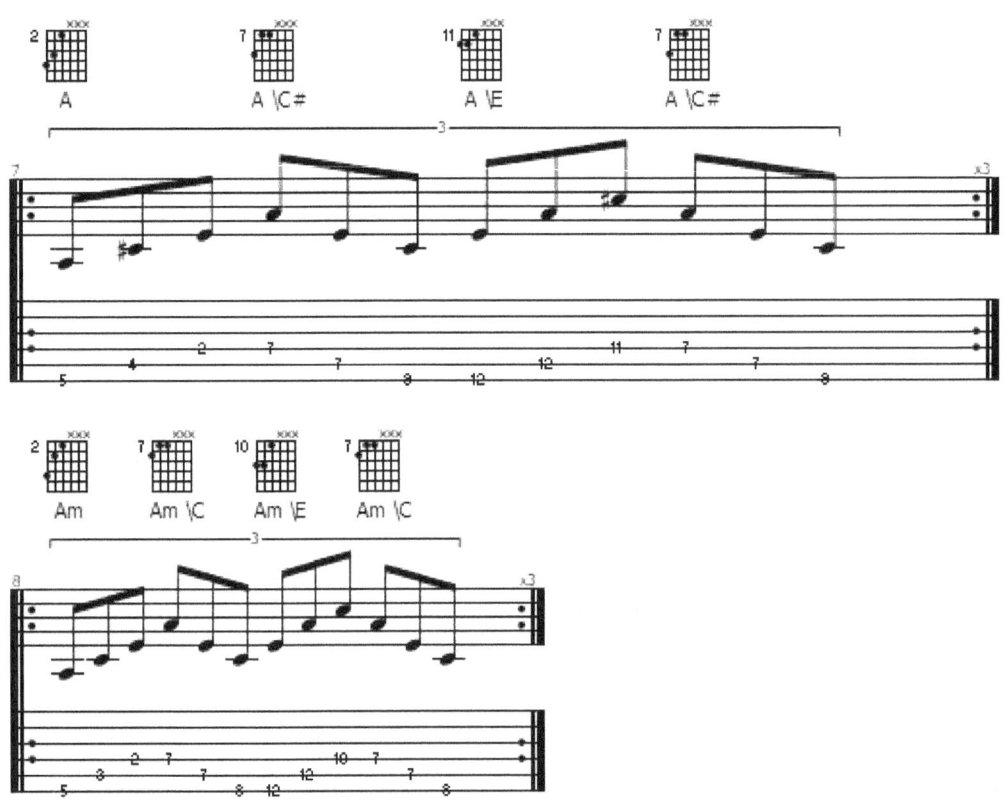

Set 4 Harmonized Scale Chord Inversion

Chapter 3

Chapter 3: Understanding Scales on Guitar

Chapter 3:1 Some Basic Scale forms - Moving easily from chord to chord.

    2 String Scales Major & Minor & Pentatonic

    3 String Scales Major & Minor

    4 to 6 String Scales Major & Minor & Pentatonic

Chapter 3:2 Harmonized Scales - Sounding big and easy to control.

    Scales in 3rds

    Scales in 6ths

    Scales in Octaves

    Scales in 10ths

Chapter 3:3 Diatonic Harmonized Scales - Arranging made easy.

    Any scale major, minor, blues, pentatonic, can be harmonized.

    Chords are placed on each step of the scale and used like playing scales,

    taking you away from just hearing 1-4-5 chord progressions.

    Harmonized scales give you a tool to develop and thicken your arrangement,

    to compete with a studio version of a song with 64 tracks of sound.

Two String Major Scale Form
(All Slides on First Finger)

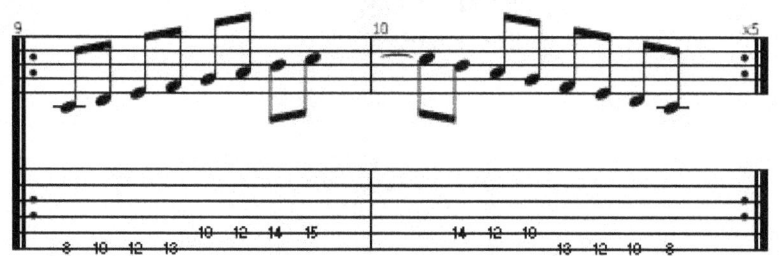

Two String Minor Scale Form
(All Slides on First Finger)

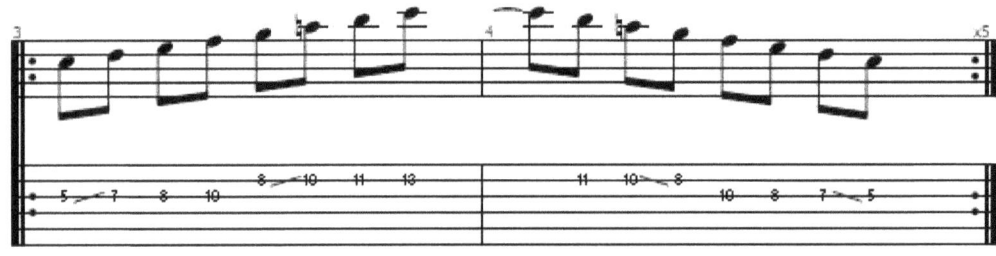
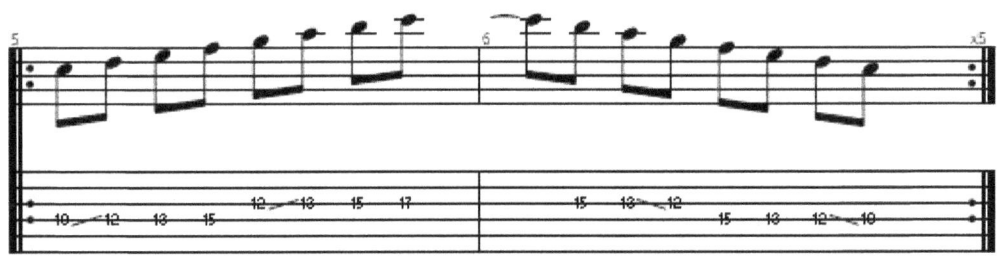
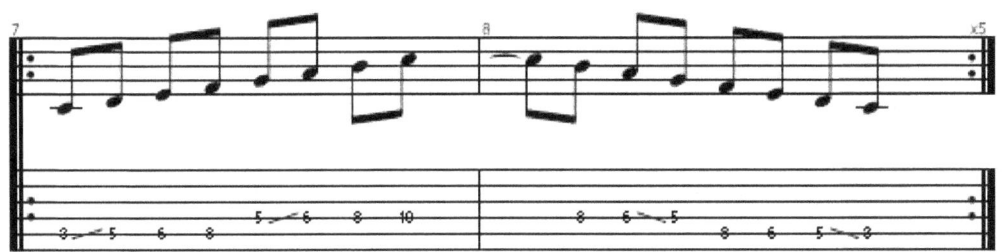

Two String Dorian Mode Scale Form

(Two String Dorian Mode Scale Form)

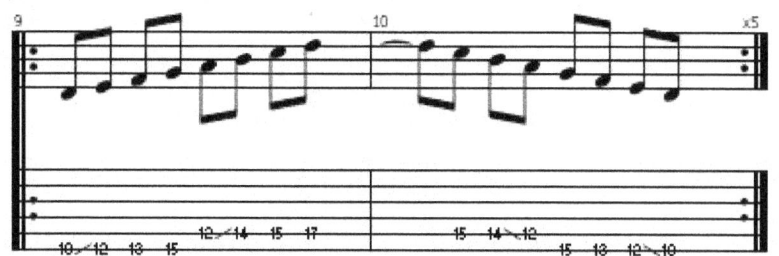

Three String Major Scale Form

Three String Minor Scale Form

(Three String Minor Scale Form)

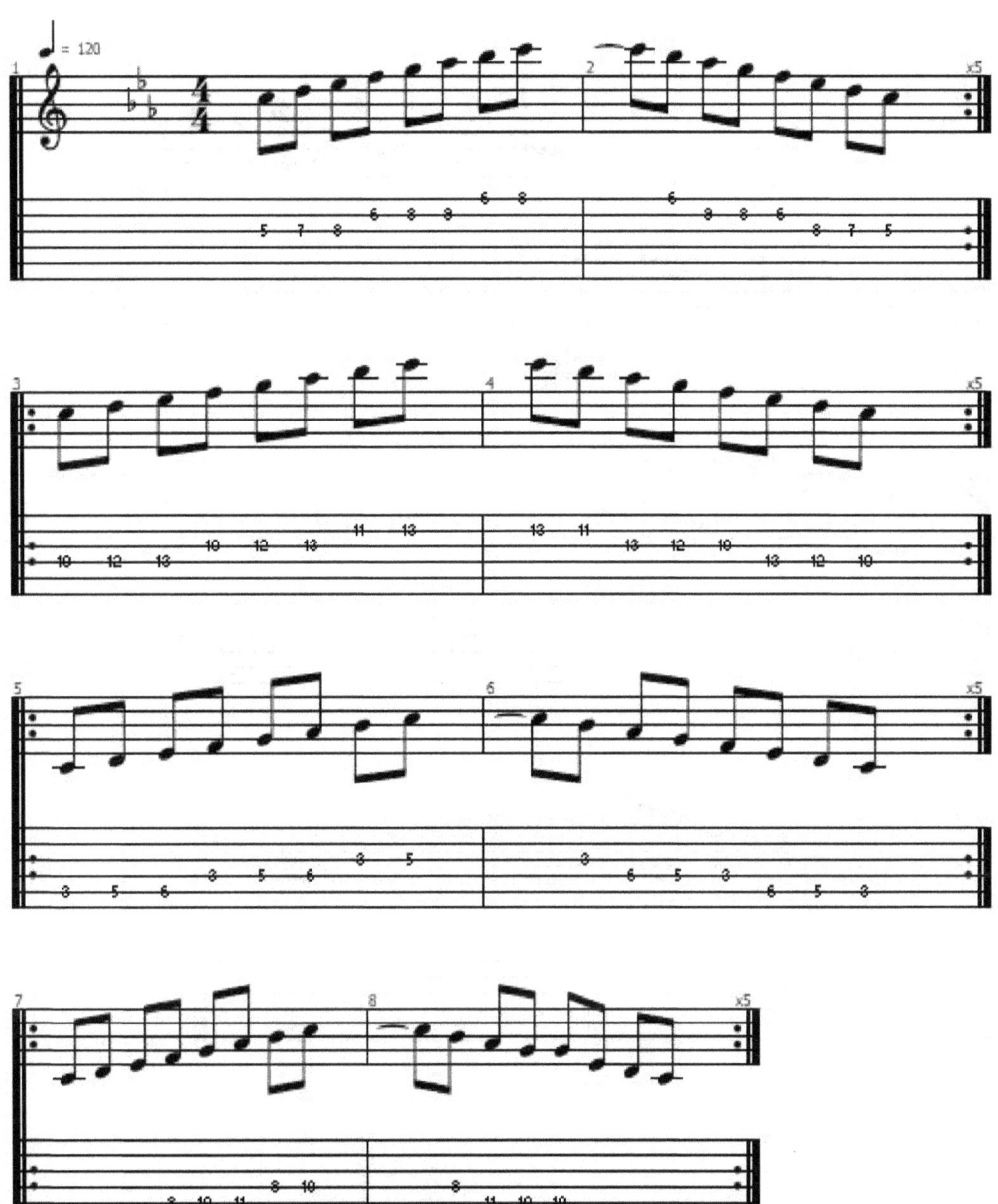

Major Scales in 3rds

C Major Scale

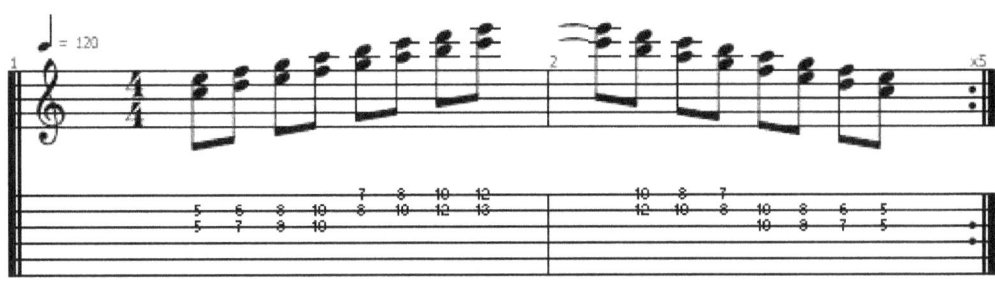

G Major Scale

F Major Scale

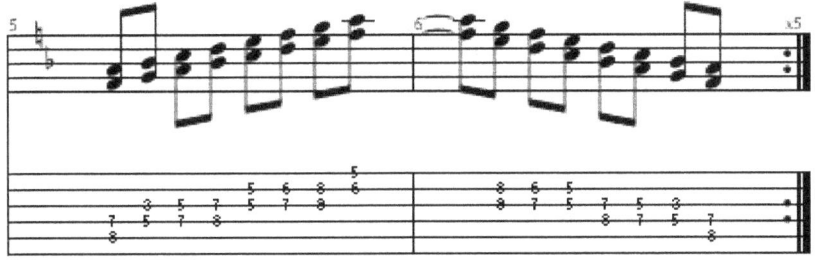

Major Scales in 6th form 1 & 2

(Major Scale in 6th form 1&2)

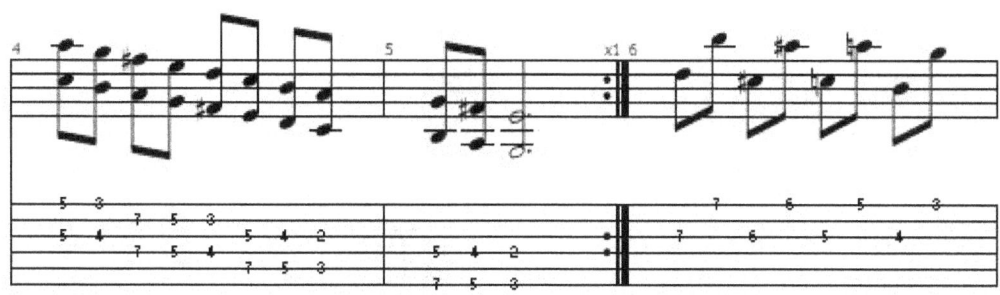

Major Scales in Octaves form 1&2

(Major Scales in Octaves)

Major Scale in 10th s Form 1&2

Major Scale in 10th's Form 1&2

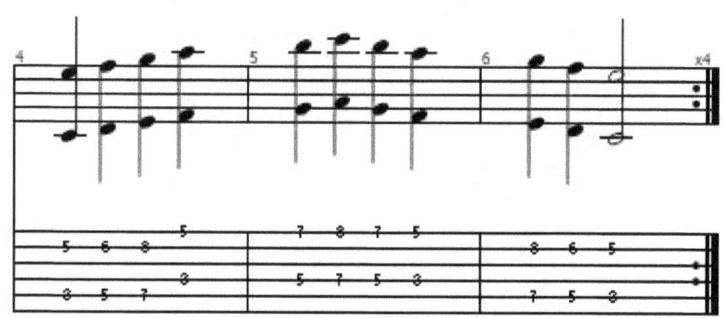

Pentatonic scales
(Pentatonic Double Stops)

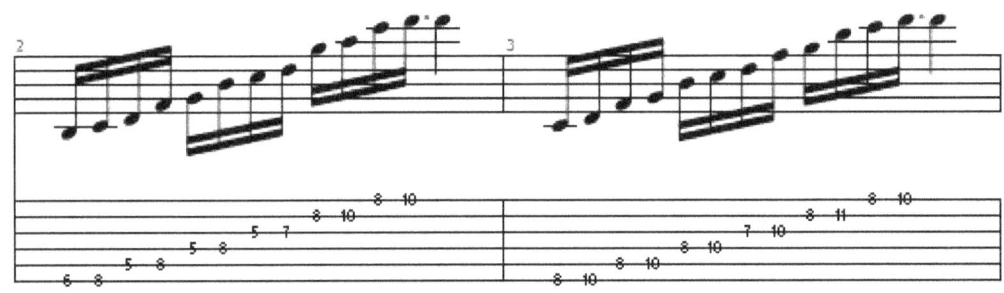

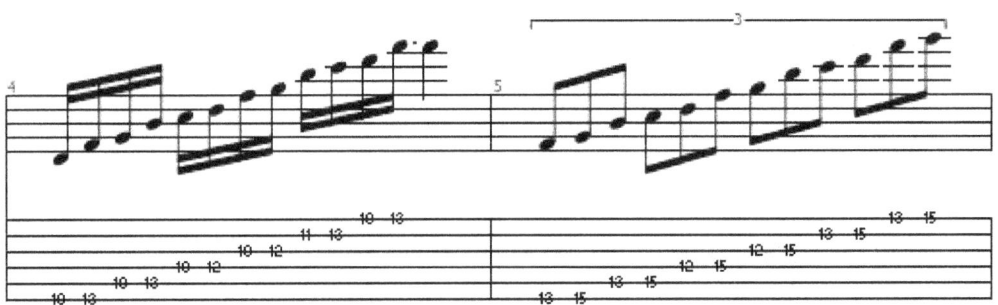

Chapter 4

Chapter 4: **Copy Players you like. You will learn faster.**

Chapter 4:1 Five players you like.

Chapter 4:2 Finger Style you like

Chapter 4:3 Pick Style you like

Chapter 4:4 Pick and Fingerstyle you like

Questions

What do your five favorite players have in common ?

Are they a classical fingerstyle?

Are they a folk fingerstyle?

Do they only play with a pick?

Do they play with a pick and fingers?

Are they all rock or folk or jazz or country?

Chapter 5

Chapter 5: **Pedal Tones** (Pedal Point)

Chapter 5:1 What is a pedal tone? Any tone prolonged throughout changes in harmony.

In music, a pedal point is a sustained tone, typically in the bass, during which at least one foreign harmony is sounded in the other parts. A pedal point sometimes functions as a non-chord tone, placing it in the categories alongside suspension, retardations and passing tones.

Chapter 5:2 Why would you use it?

Pedal tones are common throughout all music styles, they are prominent in commercial music.

Pedal Tone Study
(Key of D Major)

In Conclusion

If you watch and listen to your favorite players, you will more than likely hear most of this book. Play each music exercise until it's easy and try them in different keys. Know your fingerboard and vocabulary. This is not new knowledge, just less used and practiced by guitar hobbyists. I hope this book brings more into your Musical Life!

Perry Howell

www.ingramcontent.com/pod-product-compliance
Lightning Source LLC
Chambersburg PA
CBHW080350170426
43194CB00014B/2743